The David Series #1

Faithful and Fearless: Parents' & Teachers' Manual

Co-Written by
Dr. Veronica Amaku
Dr. Samuel Amaku

A Parents' & Teachers' Companion Manual to "Fearless"

Ambassador Publishing

RAISING FOUNDATIONS OF MANY GENERATIONS

Copyright © 2024 by Veronica Amaku

Published in 2024 by Ambassador Publishing. All rights reserved. No part of this book may be used or reproduced in any manner whatsoever without written permission except in the case of brief quotations embodied in critical articles and reviews

Book Design by Toluwanimi Babarinde

Inks by Jadyn Richardson

Send inquiries to ambassador.publish@gmail.com

This coloring and activity book accompanies each volume of the David series.

The David Series is a collection of children's books that feature the biblical David as the protagonist. The goal is to inspire young readers through relatable, captivating stories highlighting David's courage, perseverance, failures, and faith. To keep children engaged, we incorporated an art style that is highly adept at evoking emotions and bridging the gap between classic and modern tales. Furthermore, the illustrations' inclusive nature promote diversity and expose youngsters to different artistic styles and cultures, cultivating a deep appreciation for the arts.

ISBN: 978-0-9788390-7-9

Order the Picture books here - https://bit.ly/davidanswers

or scan the QR code below:

Introduction

Welcome to Faithful and Fearless: A Parents' and Teacher's companion manual to "Fearless," a resource designed to equip homeschooling teachers, Sunday school teachers, and parents with tools to accompany Fearless—A Story of Faith and Courage from Young David. Our hope is that these lessons from the life of young David will inspire courage, foster resilience, and nurture a deep connection with God in the children you teach. As it is written in Joshua 1:9, 'Be strong and courageous. Do not be afraid; do not be discouraged, for the Lord your God will be with you wherever you go,' we aim to help children find the courage and strength that comes from trusting in God.

This manual is for homeschooling educators, Sunday school teachers, and parents who are passionate about providing Bible-based education. Whether experienced or new to leading Bible studies, this guide supports making faith formation accessible and exciting for children.

Faithful and Fearless centers on Bible-based education, character development, spiritual growth, and faith formation. Each lesson and activity is rooted in David's values—courage, trust in God, perseverance, and worship. Children will learn about David's story and be encouraged to apply these values in their lives. Proverbs 3:5 reminds us to 'Trust in the Lord with all your heart and lean not on your own understanding,' emphasizing the importance of guiding children to trust God completely in all aspects of their journey.

Teaching children about God's love and promises is a special task. This manual aims to inspire and equip you with practical guidance and engaging activities. It offers creative craft projects, interactive games, reflection prompts, and music activities—all to help children understand David's life and incorporate its lessons into their experiences.

This manual is both a practical and inspirational resource, offering structured lessons, activities, and reflections to help children relate David's story to their own lives. Children will develop a strong moral foundation and an unshakable trust in God through Bible readings, discussions, crafts, games, and songs. The resources are flexible, allowing you to tailor each lesson to your children's needs.

As you journey through these lessons, remember that, like Lois and Eunice, Timothy's grandmother and mother, respectively, you are helping to plant seeds of faith that will continue to grow throughout the children's lives. By using David's story as an example of trust and courage, you provide young readers with a model for facing life's challenges with faith and strength.

We hope that this manual will inspire both the children and you—the teachers and parents—on your faith journey.

Sincerely,

Dr. Veronica Amaku

About the Authors

Dr. Veronica Amaku

Dr. Veronika Amaku, a devoted wife, mother, and college professor, inspires through unwavering faith. Born again in 1983, she actively served in campus Christian organizations and as a trained worker with Children Evangelism Ministry.

She nurtured young minds with the wisdom of the Bible by teaching Sunday schools and establishing Bible Clubs for children in Nigeria and the United States. Guided by God's grace, she raised five children who love the Lord. Her life exemplifies faith's transformative power.

Her children's books impart values of love, faith, and compassion, touching young hearts worldwide. She is a remarkable author and role model.

Dr. Samuel Amaku

Dr. Samuel Amaku brings decades of teaching expertise and an unwavering commitment to nurturing young minds as the co-author of this instructional manual. With a distinguished career spanning roles as an educator in elementary, secondary, and collegiate settings, Dr. Amaku has dedicated his life to creating impactful learning experiences that inspire critical thinking, resilience, and a love for knowledge.

Holding advanced degrees in Educational Administration and Supervision, along with multiple teaching certifications in English Language Arts and ESL, Dr. Amaku has a proven track record of academic excellence. His philosophy of teaching centers on the holistic development of the learner, emphasizing a child-centered approach that fosters creativity, critical thinking, and problem-solving skills. He believes that education is not merely about instruction but about building environments where every student can thrive and contribute meaningfully to their community.

As a co-author of this manual, Dr. Amaku draws on his vast teaching experience, professional training, and heartfelt passion for education to create a resource that empowers teachers, parents, and caregivers. His work reflects his steadfast belief that the collaboration between educators and families can shape a generation that is not only academically capable but also morally grounded and spiritually enriched.

Lesson Plans

Overview

These lesson plans are designed to align with TEKS (Texas Essential Knowledge and Skills) and other homeschool accreditation standards, ensuring compatibility for use in private Christian schools and homeschooling environments. The goal is to teach core Biblical values such as courage, faith, and perseverance while also addressing educational standards for literacy, critical thinking, and personal development.

Grade Level: 3rd - 5th Grade

Duration: 3 Weeks (1 Lesson per Week)

Lesson 1: Introduction to David's Story

Objective

Children will learn about David's early life as a shepherd and the concept of trusting God in difficult situations.

TEKS Alignment

ELA: Reading Comprehension Skills (3.10): Analyze, make inferences, and draw conclusions about the theme and genre in different cultural, historical, and contemporary contexts.

Social Studies: History (3.1): Describe the lives of Christian leaders who exemplified qualities such as courage and faith.

Activities

1. Read Aloud: The teacher reads the first part of David's story, focusing on his duties as a shepherd and his encounter with the lion.

2. Discussion Questions:

   What qualities did David show when faced with the lion?

   How did David's trust in God help him overcome his fear?

3. Character Map Activity: Children create a character map of David, identifying his key traits (e.g., bravery, responsibility).

4. Memory Verse: Select a memory verse card from the list and assist the children to memorize the verse.

Lesson 2: Facing Challenges with Courage

Objective

Children will learn about courage and the importance of having faith during challenging situations.

TEKS Alignment

Health: Mental and Emotional Health (3.7): Identify and apply skills for managing emotions and coping with challenges.

ELA: Writing (3.11): Write literary texts to express ideas and feelings about real or imagined people, events, and ideas.

Activities

1. Creative Writing: Children write a short story about a time they faced a challenge and how they overcame it with courage.

2. Role-Playing: Children role-play the scene of David facing the lion, emphasizing the emotions and decisions involved.

3. Bible Verse Reflection: Reflect on 1 Timothy 3:16-17 and discuss how scripture can guide us in difficult times.

4. Memory Verse: Select a memory verse card from the list and assist the children to memorize the verse.

Lesson 3: Trusting in God's Plan

Objective:

Children will understand the value of trusting God's plan and recognizing His protection in everyday life.

TEKS Alignment

ELA: Listening and Speaking (3.3): Listen actively to interpret a message and ask clarifying questions when needed.

Social Studies: Citizenship (3.9): Identify examples of responsible decision-making in family life and community situations.

Activities

1. Group Discussion: Discuss David's decision to face the lion instead of running away. How does this decision show trust in God?

2. Art Activity: Children illustrate a scene from the story that shows God's protection over David.

3. Prayer Journal: Encourage children to write a prayer thanking God for His protection and sharing a personal challenge where they need His guidance.

4. Memory Verse: Select a memory verse card from the list and assist the children to memorize the verse.

Lesson Assessments

Formative: Participation in discussions, creative writing activities, and character maps.

Summative: Completion of prayer journals, illustrations, and group discussions to assess understanding of key concepts such as courage and trust in God.

Materials Needed for the lessons

1. The David Series #1: "Fearless - A Story of Faith and Courage from Young David"
2. Art supplies (paper, crayons, markers)
3. Writing journals

Reflection for Teachers and Parents

Each lesson is designed to educate and nurture the child's spiritual growth. Encourage children to relate the lessons to their own lives and see David's story as a model for trusting God and being courageous in the face of adversity.

Activity Worksheets

Comprehension Worksheet

Objective

Assess children's understanding of David's story and the moral lessons within it.

Sample Questions

(Feel free to come up with your own questions):

1. Who was David, and what were his responsibilities as a young shepherd?
2. How did David react when he saw the lion approaching the sheep?
3. What qualities did David show when facing the lion?
4. How did David's trust in God help him overcome his fear?
5. What lesson can we learn from David's story about facing challenges?

Activity

Children will answer questions individually and then share their answers in small groups to discuss different perspectives.

Drawing and Coloring Activity

Objective

Encourage children to visualize the story of David through art.

Activity

- For younger children: Provide coloring pages depicting scenes from the story. Coloring Book to accompany the book is available for purchase as a separate resource (Coloring book to accompany Fearless: A Story of Faith and Courage from Young David ISBN: 978-0-9788390-5-5)

- For older children: Encourage their inner creativity by allowing them to draw and color their favorite scenes from the story, such as David playing his harp for the sheep or facing the lion.

Discussion Prompt

Ask children to explain why they chose that particular scene and what it means to them.

Sequencing Activity

Objective

Help children understand the sequence of events in David's story.

Activity

Provide children with cut-out strips containing key events from the story.

Children will arrange the events in the correct order and then paste them onto a worksheet.

Key Events to Include:

1. David caring for his sheep.
2. David notices the lion approaching.
3. David praying for strength.
4. David uses his sling to strike the lion.
5. David thanking God for His protection.

Reflection Worksheet

Objective

Encourage children to think about how they can apply the story's lessons to their own lives.

Prompts

1. Describe a time when you had to be brave. What did you do?
2. How can you trust God when you face something that scares you?
3. Write a prayer asking God to help you be brave like David.

Vocabulary Practice Worksheet

Objective

Introduce children to new vocabulary words from the story and improve language skills.

Words to Include: Courage, perseverance, shepherd, predator, protection, faith, pasture.

Activities

Match the Word: Match vocabulary words to their definitions.

Fill in the Blank: Use the vocabulary words to complete sentences related to the story.

Character Analysis Worksheet

Objective

Analyze David's character traits and understand their importance.

Activity

Character Traits: List David's character traits, such as bravery, trust in God, and responsibility.

Examples from the Story: Provide examples from the story that demonstrate each trait.

Discussion: Discuss why these traits were important for David and how we can show them in our own lives.

Crossword Puzzle

Objective

Reinforce key vocabulary and events in a fun and engaging way.

Activity

Refer to the activity book accompanying Fearless – A Story of Faith and Courage from Young David (ISBN:) and select an age-appropriate crossword puzzle for the children.

Creative Writing Prompt

Objective

Allow children to express their creativity by imagining themselves in David's position.

Activity

Prompt: Imagine you are David, standing in front of the lion. Write about what you are thinking and feeling in that moment. How do you find the courage to face the lion?

Sharing: Children can share their writing with a partner or in small groups.

Materials Needed for the activities

- Drawing paper, crayons, markers
- Scissors, glue sticks
- Worksheets with comprehension questions, vocabulary exercises, and reflection prompts
- Crossword puzzle templates

Reflection for Teachers and Parents:

These worksheets are designed to reinforce the key lessons from David's story in fun and engaging ways. Encourage children to share their thoughts and drawings and use these activities as a springboard for deeper discussions about faith, courage, and trusting God in difficult situations.

Memory Verse Cards

Overview

These memory verse cards are designed to help children memorize and internalize key Bible verses that reinforce the themes of faith, courage, and trust in God, as illustrated in David's story. Teachers, parents, or children can use them independently for reflection and learning.

Format

- Each card includes a Bible verse, an illustration, and a discussion prompt.
- Cards are sized for easy printing (4"x6").

Memory Verses

1 Samuel 17:37 (NLT) - "The Lord who rescued me from the claws of the lion and the bear will rescue me from this Philistine!"

Illustration: David standing confidently before the lion.

Discussion Prompt: How did David trust God to protect him? What can you trust God for today?

Psalm 28:7 (NLT) - "The Lord is my strength and shield. I trust him with all my heart. He helps me, and my heart is filled with joy."

Illustration: David playing the harp, surrounded by his sheep.

Discussion Prompt: How can trusting God help us feel joyful, even when we're scared?

Proverbs 3:5-6 (NLT) - "Trust in the Lord with all your heart; do not depend on your own understanding. Seek his will in all you do, and he will show you which path to take."

Illustration: David praying before facing the lion.

Discussion Prompt: What does it mean to trust God with all your heart?

Psalm 23:1 (NLT) - "The Lord is my shepherd; I have all that I need."

Illustration: David caring for his sheep in a lush green pasture.

Discussion Prompt: How is God like a shepherd to us, just as David was to his sheep?

Joshua 1:9 (NLT) - "This is my command—be strong and courageous! Do not be afraid or discouraged. For the Lord your God is with you wherever you go."

Illustration: David standing with his sling, ready to face the lion.

Discussion Prompt: When do you need to be courageous? How does knowing that God is with you help?

Activities Using Memory Verse Cards

1. Memory Game:

Lay out the cards face down. Children take turns flipping two cards at a time, trying to match the illustration to the correct verse. This helps reinforce both the imagery and the scripture.

2. Verse Recitation Practice:

Have the children work in pairs. One child reads the verse aloud, while the other closes their eyes and tries to repeat it from memory. This encourages teamwork and retention.

3. Verse of the Week:

Choose one card each week as the focus. Encourage children to reflect on the verse throughout the week and discuss how they can apply it in their daily lives.

4. Story Connection:

After reading Fearless: The Story of Faith and Courage from Young David, connect the key events from the story to the memory verses. Have children choose a verse that best reflects David's actions and explain why.

Materials Needed for Memory Verse Card Activity

- Printable cardstock for memory verse cards.
- Crayons or markers for coloring illustrations (if providing uncolored versions).
- Laminator (optional) for durability.

Reflection for Teachers and Parents

These memory verse cards are meant to help children internalize Biblical principles in an interactive and engaging way. Use them regularly to help children memorize scripture and understand how the lessons apply to their lives.

Role-playing Scripts

Overview

These role-playing scripts are designed to help children imagine themselves in the shoes of David and other characters from the story, enabling them to better understand the emotions, decisions, and faith behind David's actions. They are ideal for use in classrooms, Sunday schools, or at home, offering a dynamic way to bring the story to life and reinforce its key messages.

Format

- Each script includes multiple roles (David, Narrator, Sheep, Lion, David's Brothers, etc.) and simple dialogue to make it easy for young children to understand and perform.
- Scripts are short (5-10 minutes) and designed for groups of 4-6 children.

Role-Playing Scenarios

Scenario 1: David Protects the Sheep

Characters: Narrator, David, Sheep, Lion

Setting: A lush green pasture at sunset.

Script

Narrator: "One evening, David was herding his sheep to a safe place to graze. The sun was setting, and everything seemed peaceful."

Sheep: "Baaa, baa! We love this green grass, David!"

David: (smiling) "Eat well, my friends. I will watch over you."

Narrator: "Suddenly, David heard rustling in the bushes. He knew this could be dangerous. He prayed silently for God's protection."

Lion: (growling softly) "I see some sheep. Dinner time!"

David: (firmly) "Not today! I will protect my sheep! God is with me!"

Narrator: "David bravely stood in front of the sheep, picked up his sling, and faced the lion. He trusted God to help him."

David: (swinging the sling) "Go away, lion! These sheep are under my care."

Lion: (pausing, startled) "This human is brave... I think I'll leave."

Narrator: "The lion turned away, and the sheep were safe. David thanked God for His strength and courage."

David: (bowing his head) "Thank you, Lord, for being my strength and protector."

Scenario 2: David and His Brothers

Characters: Narrator, David, Brother 1, Brother 2

Setting: David's home, where his brothers are gathered.

Script

Narrator: "David was the youngest of his family. His older brothers often asked him to take care of the chores."

Brother 1: (pointing) "David, go look after the sheep while we go meet our friends."

Brother 2: (teasing) "Yes, little shepherd, make sure none of them get lost!"

David: (smiling kindly) "I will take care of them. God helps me, and I am happy to do my duty."

Narrator: "David always listened to his brothers without complaining. He knew that caring for the sheep was an important responsibility."

Brother 1: (surprised) "David, you're always so willing to help."

David: "God gives me strength to do what I need to do."

Scenario 3: David Prays for Courage

Characters: Narrator, David

Setting: A quiet spot near the pasture where David often prayed.

Script

Narrator: "David often found time to pray when he was watching over the sheep. He knew that God was always listening."

David: (kneeling down) "Dear Lord, thank you for watching over me and my sheep. Please give me courage to face any danger that comes my way."

Narrator: "David felt peace in his heart after he prayed. He knew that God was always with him."

David: (smiling) "With God by my side, I am never afraid."

Activities to Extend Role-playing

Discussion After Role-Playing:

After the role-play, gather the children and ask them how it felt to be David or one of his brothers. Discuss the emotions David must have experienced and how trusting in God helped him stay courageous.

Create Your Own Ending:

Allow children to create their own ending to the lion encounter. Ask them, "What would you do if you were David? How would you protect the sheep?" This encourages creativity and deeper thinking about the story's message.

Act It Out for Parents:

Encourage children to practice the role-play at home and perform it for their parents. This helps reinforce the lessons learned and allows parents to engage in the child's learning experience.

Materials Needed for Role-playing activities

Simple props (e.g., a small stuffed lion, a toy harp, a cloth sling) to make the role-play more interactive.

Costumes (optional): Simple costumes like a shepherd's cloak or headscarf can help children feel more connected to their roles.

Reflection for Teachers and Parents:

Role-playing helps children actively engage with the story, allowing them to internalize the lessons of faith, courage, and responsibility in a dynamic way. Encourage children to express their emotions during the role-play and discuss how trusting God made a difference in David's actions.

Bible Study Guide

Overview

This Bible study guide is designed to help children and their families or teachers dive deeper into the lessons found in David's story. It will explore the themes of courage, faith, and trusting God while relating these themes to children's everyday experiences. The guide can be used in Sunday school, homeschooling, or family devotion settings.

Structure

Each session includes a Bible reading, discussion questions, an activity, and a prayer.

The guide is divided into three sessions, each focusing on a different aspect of David's story.

Session 1: David the Shepherd

Bible Reading: 1 Samuel 16:10-13 (David's anointing) and John 10:14 (Jesus as the Good Shepherd)

Discussion Questions:

1. What was David's job as a shepherd? How did he care for his sheep?
2. What qualities make a good shepherd? How is Jesus like a shepherd for us?
3. Why do you think God chose David, the youngest son, to be anointed as king?

Activity:

Sheep Craft: Create a sheep using cotton balls and construction paper. As you craft, discuss why the sheep trusted David and how we can trust Jesus as our shepherd.

Prayer: "Dear Lord, thank you for being our Good Shepherd. Help us trust you like the sheep trusted David. Guide us in everything we do. Amen."

Session 2: Facing the Lion

Bible Reading: 1 Samuel 17:34-37 (David talks about protecting his sheep) and Psalm 23:4 (Trusting God in danger)

Discussion Questions:

1. What happened when the lion approached David's sheep?
2. How did David find the courage to face the lion?
3. Have you ever faced something scary? How can trusting God help you in these times?

Activity:

Lion Mask: Use a paper plate and crayons to make a lion mask. Afterward, have the children share how David's courage helped him face the lion and how they can face challenges with courage.

Prayer: "Lord, thank you for giving us courage when we are afraid. Help us face challenges with bravery, knowing that you are always with us. Amen."

Session 3: Trusting God's Plan

Bible Reading: Proverbs 3:5-6 (Trusting God) and 1 Samuel 17:45-47 (David's faith in God when facing Goliath)

Discussion Questions:

1. Why was David able to trust God so completely when he faced dangers?
2. What can we learn from David about trusting God even when things seem hard?
3. How can we trust God in our own lives, like David did?

Activity:

Faith Collage: Create a collage of things that represent trust and faith in God. Encourage children to find pictures from magazines or draw images that remind them of how God helps us.

Prayer: "Dear God, help us to trust you with all our hearts, just like David did. Thank you for always being there to protect and guide us. Amen."

Additional Activities

Memory Verse Practice: Practice memorizing Psalm 23:1, "The Lord is my shepherd; I have all that I need." Encourage children to share the verse with their family members.

Song and Worship: Sing "He's Got the Whole World in His Hands" to remind children of God's care and protection, just like David experienced with his sheep.

Reflection Journal: Encourage children to keep a journal of times when they trusted God and what happened as a result. This helps them see how God works in their lives, just as He worked in David's life.

Materials Needed:

- Construction paper, glue, scissors, crayons, cotton balls
- Magazines for collages, paper plates for masks
- Journals for children to record reflections

Reflection for Teachers and Parents:

This Bible study guide is intended to help children internalize the lessons of faith, courage, and trust that David's story teaches. By diving deeper into these themes through activities, crafts, and discussions, children can relate the lessons of David to their own lives, seeing how God is with them every day, just as He was with David.

Interactive Games

Overview:

These interactive games are designed to help children engage more deeply with the story of David by reinforcing key themes like courage, faith, and trusting God. They are intended for use in Sunday school, homeschooling, or family activities to make learning about the Bible fun and memorable.

Game Ideas:

Courage Quest Board Game

Objective:

Help children understand the importance of courage and trusting God in challenging situations, just as David did.

Setup:

Create a simple board game path with various challenges represented by different colored spaces.

Players move along the path by rolling a die and drawing challenge cards.

Gameplay:

Each player takes turns rolling the die to move forward.

When landing on a challenge space, the player must draw a card, answer a question, or complete a task.

Examples of challenges:

Faith Challenge: "Name a time you had to be brave. How did you feel?"

David's Courage Task: "Pretend you are David facing the lion. Show us your brave face!"

Winning: The first player to reach the end of the path wins, but all players should be encouraged for their bravery along the journey.

David's Sling Toss

Objective:

Reinforce the concept of how David used his skills to protect the sheep and trust in God's power.

Setup:

Use bean bags or small soft balls to represent stones and set up a target (such as a cardboard cutout of a lion).

Children take turns tossing the "stones" to hit the target.

Gameplay:

Each child gets three attempts to hit the target.

When a child hits the target, encourage them by saying, "Just like David, you showed courage and faith!"

After each turn, discuss how God helps us face challenges, no matter how big they seem.

Memory Verse Matching Game

Objective:

Help children memorize key Bible verses from the story of David.

Setup:

Create cards with Bible verses and matching illustrations from the story.

Mix up the cards and lay them face down.

Gameplay:

Children take turns flipping over two cards at a time, trying to match the verse to its corresponding illustration.

When a match is found, read the verse aloud and discuss its meaning.

Continue until all matches are found.

Trust Walk

Objective

Teach children about the importance of trusting God and others, just as David trusted God to guide him.

Setup:

Create an obstacle course using household items or classroom materials.

Pair children together and give one child a blindfold.

Gameplay:

One child wears the blindfold while the other guides them through the obstacle course by giving verbal directions.

Discuss how it felt to trust someone else and relate it to trusting God in our own lives.

Shepherd's Call Game

Objective:

Reinforce the idea that Jesus, like David, is our shepherd, and we need to listen to His voice.

Setup:

Choose one child to be the "Shepherd" and the others to be the "Sheep."

The "Shepherd" calls out commands, such as "Come here, sheep!" or "Stop, sheep!" while the other children follow the instructions.

Gameplay:

The game can be played in an open space where the sheep try to follow the Shepherd's command.

After the game, discuss how we need to listen to Jesus and follow Him, just like the sheep listen to the shepherd.

Materials Needed:

Board game supplies (dice, game pieces, challenge cards)

Bean bags or small soft balls, cardboard cutout for sling toss target

Cards with Bible verses and illustrations for matching game

Blindfolds and household items for the obstacle course

Reflection for Teachers and Parents:

These interactive games are designed to reinforce the key messages from "Fearless—A Story of Faith and Courage from Young David" in a fun and engaging way. By playing these games, children will not only enjoy learning but also internalize the important lessons of courage, faith, and trust in God. Encourage children to relate their experiences in the games to real-life situations where they can demonstrate courage and faith in God.

Family Devotional Guide

Overview:

This family devotional guide is designed to help families explore the lessons from David's story together. It includes activities, discussion questions, and reflections that foster meaningful conversations about faith, courage, and trusting God. This guide can be used during family devotion times, providing a structured way for families to grow spiritually together.

Structure:

- The guide is divided into three devotion sessions, each focusing on a specific lesson from David's story.
- Each session includes a Bible reading, discussion prompts, a family activity, and a prayer.

Session 1: David's Trust in God

Bible Reading: 1 Samuel 17:34-37 (David talks to Saul about his courage and trust in God when facing the lion and the bear)

Discussion Prompts:

1. Why do you think David was able to trust God when he faced the lion?
2. How can we trust God when we face difficult or scary situations?
3. What are some things God has helped our family overcome?

Family Activity:

Family Courage Story: Each family member shares a time when they felt scared but found the courage to face the situation. Write these stories down or create simple drawings to remind everyone that God is always there to help us.

Prayer: "Dear God, thank you for always being with us, just like you were with David. Help us trust you and be brave when we face challenges. Amen."

Session 2: God's Protection

Bible Reading: Psalm 23:4 (David's confidence in God's protection) and Proverbs 18:10 (The Lord as a strong tower)

Discussion Prompts:

1. How does God protect us, just like David protected his sheep?
2. What are some ways we can feel safe when we remember God is with us?
3. How can we remind each other that God is our protector?

Family Activity:

God's Shield Craft: Create a shield out of cardboard or construction paper. Decorate it with words or symbols that represent God's protection (e.g., a cross, a heart, or the word "courage"). Hang it up somewhere in your home as a reminder.

Prayer: "Lord, thank you for being our protector and shield. Help us always remember that we are safe because you are with us. Amen."

Session 3: The Power of Faith

Bible Reading: 1 Samuel 17:45-47 (David declares his faith in God before facing Goliath)

Discussion Prompts:

1. What gave David the confidence to stand up to Goliath?
2. How does having faith in God help us when we face difficult situations?
3. How can we encourage each other to trust God more?

Family Activity:

Faith Jar: Create a "Faith Jar" for your family. Whenever someone in the family faces a challenge and overcomes it by trusting God, write it down on a slip of paper and add it to the jar. Over time, read the slips together to remind each other of God's faithfulness.

Prayer: "Dear God, help us to have strong faith like David did. Give us courage to face the things that seem too big for us, knowing that you are always with us. Amen."

Additional Family Activities:

1. Memory Verse Practice:

Memorize Proverbs 3:5-6 together as a family: "Trust in the Lord with all your heart; do not depend on your own understanding. Seek his will in all you do, and he will show you which path to take."

Make it fun by turning it into a song or using hand motions.

2. Storytelling Time:

Have a storytelling evening where each family member retells their favorite part of David's story. Discuss why that part was special to them and what they learned from it.

3. Family Praise Session:

Gather to sing songs about trusting God, such as "Trust and Obey" or "He's Got the Whole World in His Hands." Use this time to praise God for all He has done for your family.

Materials Needed:

Construction paper, markers, glue, and cardboard for crafts

Slips of paper and a jar for the Faith Jar

Journals for family members to write down reflections (optional)

Reflection for Families:

This devotional guide is meant to strengthen the faith of the entire family by creating opportunities for open discussion and shared experiences. Use these sessions to not only learn from David's story but also to grow closer as a family, supporting and encouraging one another in your walk with God.

Story-Themed Craft Projects

Overview: These craft projects are designed to help children connect more deeply with the story of David through hands-on activities. Each craft project ties into a key theme from the story, allowing children to express their creativity while internalizing the lessons of faith, courage, and trust in God. These crafts can be done in Sunday school, homeschool, or family settings.

Craft Projects:

David's Sling Craft

Objective: To help children visualize David's bravery by creating their own slings.

Materials Needed:

- Felt or fabric strips (for the sling strap)
- A small pouch or piece of fabric (to represent the stone holder)
- Markers, glue, scissors

Instructions:

- Cut a strip of felt or fabric to serve as the sling strap.
- Attach a small pouch or piece of fabric to the end of the strap to hold "stones."
- Decorate the sling with symbols of courage and faith, such as a cross or a heart.

Discussion:

Talk about how David used his sling with God's help and how we can be brave in our own lives when God is with us.

Sheep Puppet Craft

Objective: To reinforce David's role as a shepherd and how he cared for his sheep.

Materials Needed:

- Paper lunch bags
- Cotton balls
- Markers, glue, construction paper

Instructions:

Use the paper lunch bag as the base for the sheep puppet.

Glue cotton balls all over the front to create a fluffy sheep.

Draw a face on the sheep using markers or cut out shapes from construction paper.

Discussion:

Discuss how David took care of his sheep and how God takes care of us like a shepherd.

Courage Crown

Objective: To celebrate David's courage and remind children that they, too, can be brave.

Materials Needed:

- Construction paper (different colors)
- Stickers, markers, glue, scissors
- Glitter (optional)

Instructions:

- Cut out a strip of construction paper long enough to wrap around a child's head.
- Decorate the strip with words like "Brave," "Faithful," and "Courageous," along with stickers and other embellishments.
- Tape or glue the ends together to form a crown.

Discussion:

Talk about how David showed courage and how we can wear our "crown of courage" by trusting God in difficult situations.

Shield of Faith Craft

Objective: To emphasize God's protection, just as David trusted God to protect him from danger.

Materials Needed:

Cardboard or heavy construction paper

Markers, foil, glue, scissors

Instructions:

Cut out a shield shape from cardboard or heavy construction paper.

Cover the shield with foil to give it a metallic look.

Decorate the shield with symbols that represent God's protection (e.g., a cross, a heart, or Bible verses).

Discussion:

Talk about how God protected David and how He protects us today. Encourage children to think of times when they felt God's protection.

Faith Stones

Objective: To remind children of David's faith when he chose five smooth stones to face Goliath.

Materials Needed:

Smooth river stones (or craft stones)

Paint, paintbrushes

Markers

Instructions:

Have children select five smooth stones and paint them in bright colors.

Once dry, write words like "Faith," "Courage," "Trust," "Strength," and "God" on each stone.

Discussion:

Talk about how David used the stones with faith in God, and how we can carry "stones" of faith and courage in our hearts.

David's Harp Craft

Objective: To celebrate David's musical talents and his love for praising God.

Materials Needed:

Cardboard (for the harp frame)

Rubber bands

Markers, glue, scissors

Instructions:

- Cut out a simple harp shape from cardboard.
- Stretch rubber bands across the harp frame to create "strings."
- Decorate the harp with colorful designs and symbols.

Discussion:

Talk about how David played his harp to praise God, and how we can use music to worship and thank God.

Reflection for Teachers and Parents:

These craft projects are designed to not only be fun but also meaningful. They help children internalize the story of David in creative ways, making the lessons of faith, courage, and trust in God tangible. Encourage children to share their crafts with their family members and discuss what they learned from each activity.

Reflection Journal

Overview:

This reflection journal is designed to help children process and internalize the lessons from David's story in a personal way. It includes prompts that encourage children to think about how David's experiences relate to their own lives, promoting faith, courage, and trust in God. This journal can be used at home, in Sunday school, or during family devotion times.

How to Use This Journal:

- Encourage children to take a few minutes each day or week to reflect on the prompts.
- They can write, draw, or use a combination of both to express their thoughts.
- Parents or teachers can also participate by discussing the journal entries with the children.

Journal Prompts:

1. David the Brave Shepherd

Prompt: David took care of his sheep and protected them from danger. Draw a picture of David with his sheep. How do you think David felt when he saw the lion? Write about a time when you felt scared but trusted God to help you.

2. Facing Challenges with Courage

Prompt: David trusted God and faced the lion to protect his sheep. What is a challenge you have faced recently? Write or draw about it. How did you find the courage to deal with it? How can God help you the next time you are scared?

3. God's Protection

Prompt: David knew that God was protecting him, just like a shepherd protects his sheep. Draw a picture of something that reminds you of God's protection. Write about a time when you felt God was keeping you safe.

4. Trusting God Like David

Prompt: David trusted God even when things were difficult. Write about something that is hard for you to do. How can you trust God to help you? Draw a picture of David being brave and think about how you can be brave too.

5. Faith Stones

Prompt: David picked up five stones to face Goliath, trusting in God's power. Draw a picture of the five stones David chose. Write down five things that you can do to show your faith in God. Each stone can represent one thing.

6. Praising God Like David

Prompt: David loved to praise God by playing his harp and singing. Draw yourself doing something to praise God—maybe singing, dancing, or playing an instrument. How do you feel when you praise God? Write about why it's important to thank God for everything He has done.

7. A Letter to God

Prompt: Write a letter to God thanking Him for helping you be brave like David. Tell Him about something you are grateful for and ask Him to help you with something that makes you nervous.

8. Your Own Story of Courage

Prompt: David's story shows us how to trust God and be courageous. Write or draw your own story of courage. Who helped you? How did you feel? How did trusting God make a difference?

9. Memory Verse Reflection

Prompt: Write down your favorite memory verse from David's story. Why is this verse important to you? How can you use this verse to help you in your everyday life?

10. Family Support

Prompt: David had support from his family and trusted God throughout his journey. Draw a picture of your family. Write about how your family helps you trust God and face challenges.

Reflection for Teachers and Parents:

This reflection journal encourages children to connect the story of David to their own experiences. Through writing and drawing, children are able to explore their emotions, articulate their fears, and celebrate their victories, all while building a stronger relationship with God. Take time to discuss their reflections and celebrate their growth in faith and courage.

Songs and Music Activities

Overview:

These songs and music activities are designed to help children connect with the story of David through music. Singing and music-making are effective ways to reinforce the lessons of courage, faith, and worship found in David's story. These activities are perfect for use in Sunday school, homeschool settings, or family devotion times, bringing David's love for praising God to life.

Music Activities:

Musical Instruments: "Praise Like David"

Objective:

Celebrate David's love for music by creating simple musical instruments to use during worship time.

Materials Needed:

- Small plastic containers (like empty yogurt cups)
- Rice, dried beans, or beads (for shakers)
- Rubber bands
- Markers, stickers for decoration

Instructions:

Fill the plastic containers halfway with rice or beans, secure the lid, and let children decorate the outside.

Stretch rubber bands over an empty box to create a makeshift harp.

Use these instruments while singing songs of praise, just like David did with his harp.

Dance Like David: "Joyful Worship Time"

Objective:

Encourage children to express their joy and praise through dance, just like David danced before the Lord.

Activity:

Play a lively worship song and invite children to dance around the room.

Encourage them to use scarves or ribbons as they dance, adding an element of visual joy.

Remind them of how David danced with all his heart, celebrating God's goodness.

Instrumental Reflection: "David's Harp Medley"

Objective:

Provide a calming worship time while reflecting on David's love for music.

Materials Needed:

A small harp or lyre (or a simple string instrument like a ukulele)

Recorded harp music (if live instruments are unavailable)

Activity:

Play gentle instrumental music in the background while children quietly reflect on the story of David.

Ask them to close their eyes, think about how David felt as he played his harp, and offer their own silent prayers to God.

Family Worship Night: "Songs of Faith and Courage"

Objective:

Bring the family together for a special worship session focusing on the lessons from David's story.

Activity:

- Choose a few songs that relate to themes from David's story, such as "Trust and Obey" or "He's Got the Whole World in His Hands."

- Have each family member share what they learned from David's story and then sing a song together.

- Use homemade instruments to add fun to the worship time.

Reflection for Teachers and Parents:

These songs and music activities are designed to make David's story come alive through joyful praise, song, and creativity. Encourage children to use music to express their love for God, just as David did. Singing and dancing can be powerful tools for helping children internalize Biblical truths and feel a deep connection with God.

Thank you!

Thank you for taking this journey with us. We hope this manual has provided you with the tools, inspiration, and guidance you need to nurture faith, courage, and spiritual growth in the young hearts you are teaching. Your dedication plays a vital role in shaping the next generation to be strong in their faith and fearless in their pursuit of God's calling.

The story of David is one of courage, trust, and devotion, and we hope that through the activities, lessons, and discussions in this guide, children have learned more than just a Bible story. We hope they have come to see themselves as part of God's bigger plan—believing that they, too, can be brave, faithful, and unwavering in their trust in Him. It is our prayer that the lessons learned here will help children grow closer to God, develop a strong character, and understand the importance of trusting God in every situation.

As you continue to teach and nurture these young hearts, remember that each moment you spend investing in their spiritual development is invaluable. Your role in helping them discover God's love and guidance is irreplaceable, and we are grateful for your dedication. We encourage you to revisit the story of David and the materials in this manual whenever you need to refresh your spirit or find new inspiration for your teaching.

We also want to remind you of the importance of praying for the children. Praying for their growth, protection, and faith is a powerful way to support their journey and invite God to work in their lives.

We would love to hear about your experiences using this guide and the impact it has had on your students or children. Visit our website at https//www.faithbasedlearning.org to stay connected and find other books in the series and more resources. Please feel free to share your stories, feedback, and even suggestions for future resources. Together, we can continue to support each other in the mission of nurturing strong, faith-filled children. You can also email us at admin@faithbasedlearning.org

Dear Lord, thank you for guiding us through this journey of faith. May the seeds of courage, trust, and love that have been planted in these young hearts grow and flourish. Bless every teacher, parent, guardian, caregiver, and child who has used this guide, and may they always remember that you are with them in every challenge they face. Amen.

Thank you again for your commitment to joining us in raising the foundations of many generations.

In His Service,

- Drs. Samuel and Veronica Amaku

Answer Key

Find the answers to the puzzles and cryptogram.

Get your copy of the coloring and activity book here:

https://bit.ly/davidanswers

or scan the QR code below:

HELP DAVID FIND HIS SHEEP
(MATTHEW 18:10-14)

JUST AS JESUS LEAVES THE NINETY-NINE TO LOOK FOR THE LOST SHEEP, HELP DAVID FIND HIS LOST SHEEP.

CROSSWORD PUZZLE

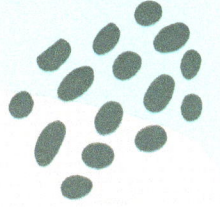

```
W I N P K S F X P H D R F M U
E F L D B D L U W B D T C W R
K E L U D F N I F J I T X L E
G A N H S A A U N O P U P Q J
N R S A T I C K X G L V E E C
D L B J O T B G O D Y S I J L
B E F D N H M S K E I I Y J C
B S A D E S B D G B A E L W O
M S I V S H V U U I C Q J U U
U O L S F E Y U O G K D P A R
O I F S W E T S B W Q G M R A
R V R Q H P D A V I D Y K A G
X T W C O K F A F C V P C Y E
Y W M B J F L I O N Q C W T M
E Y S H E P H E R D S O F J Y
```

Look for these words:

COURAGE GOD
DAVID SHEEP
FAITH STONES
LION SLING
SHEPHERDS FEARLESS

YOU CAN SEARCH FOR THEM IN DIFFERENT DIRECTIONS —
HORIZONTALLY, VERTICALLY OR DIAGONALLY

BIBLE VERSE CRYPTOGRAM

Instructions:

USE THE CODE KEY TO DECODE THE HIDDEN MESSAGE FROM A BIBLE VERSE RELATED TO THE STORY OF DAVID.

Y	V		H	G	I	L	M	T		Z	M	W
B	E		S	T	R	O	N	G		A	N	D

X	L	F	I	Z	T	V	L	F	H
C	O	U	R	A	G	E	O	U	S

U	L	I		G	S	V		O	L	I	W		R	H
F	O	R		T	H	E		L	O	R	D		I	S

D	R	G	S		B	L	F
W	I	T	H		Y	O	U

CODE KEY

A	B	C	D	E	F	G	H	I	J	K	L	M
Z	Y	X	W	V	U	T	S	R	Q	P	O	N

N	O	P	Q	R	S	T	U	V	W	X	Y	Z
M	L	K	J	I	H	G	F	E	D	C	B	A

CRISS-CROSS PUZZLE

Instructions:
1. WORDS CAN GO ACROSS OR DOWN
2. LETTERS ARE SHARE WHEN THE WORD INTERSECT

ACROSS
2. MUSICAL INSTRUMENT
4. THE SHEPHERD BOY
8. JESSE'S FAMILY TOWN
9. WEAPON OF VICTORY

DOWN
1. TRUST IN GOD
3. TALKING TO GOD
5. NUMBER OF DAVID'S SIBLINGS
6. DAVID CARED FOR THESE ANIMALS
7. KING OF KINGS

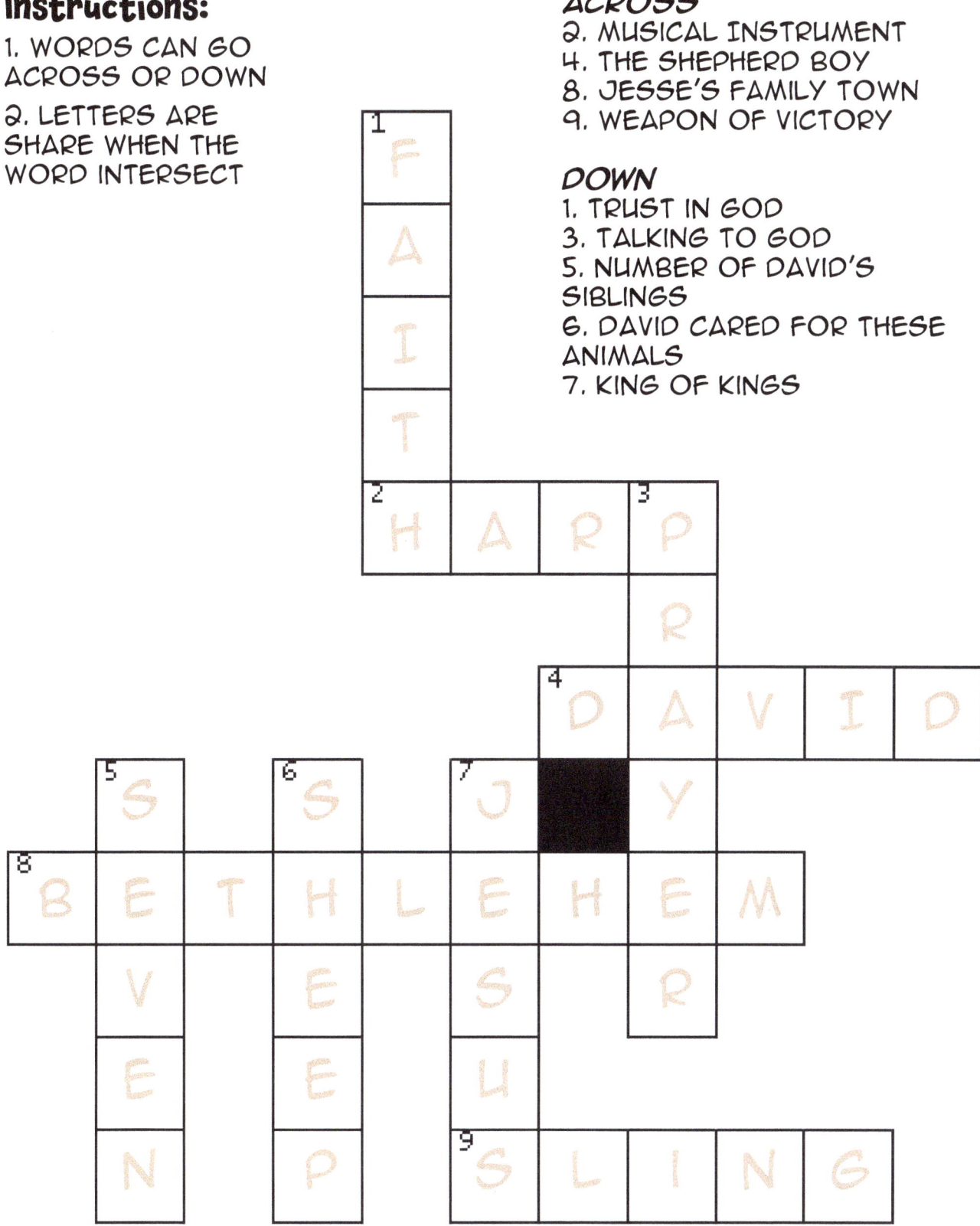

HELP DAVID REACH THE STREAM

HELP DAVID FIND A STONE FOR HIS SLING THAT HE USED TO DEFEAT THE PREDATORS AND PROTECT THE SHEEP.

www.ingramcontent.com/pod-product-compliance
Lightning Source LLC
Chambersburg PA
CBHW061816290426
44110CB00026B/2890